Moments of
Grace

Published by
The Bible Reading Fellowship
15 The Chambers, Vineyard
Abingdon OX14 3FE
United Kingdom
Tel: +44 (0)1865 319700
Email: enquiries@brf.org.uk
Website: www.brf.org.uk
BRF is a Registered Charity

ISBN 978 0 85746 224 4

First published 2013

10 9 8 7 6 5 4 3 2 1 0

Acknowledgments
Unless otherwise stated, scripture quotations are taken from the New Revised Standard
Version of the Bible, Anglicised Edition, copyright © 1989, 1995 by the Division of Christian
Education of the National Council of the Churches of Christ in the United States of America,
and are used by permission. All rights reserved.

Extracts from *A New Zealand Prayer Book / He Karakia Mihinare o Aotearoa* are reproduced by
kind permission of The Anglican Church in Aotearoa, New Zealand and Polynesia.

The paper used in the production of this publication was supplied by mills that source their
raw materials from sustainably managed forests. Soy-based inks were used in its printing and
the laminate film is biodegradable.

A catalogue record for this book is available from the British Library

Printed in Singapore by Craft Print International Ltd

Moments of Grace

Reflections on
meeting with God

Joy MacCormick

❖ ❖ ❖

To the memory of my parents,
Bernice May and Charles Allan McQuarrie,
who clothed me in humanity;
to my sons Peter and John
and grandchildren
Hayley and Olivia, Jack and Sally,
through whom I learn to love and to be loved,
this work is dedicated.

❖ ❖ ❖

Contents

Gospel moments

Pondering

Foreword

The Reverend Joy MacCormick, a Priest in the Anglican Church in Aotearoa, New Zealand and Polynesia, writes *Moments of Grace*, a collection of 40 poems, from her experience of God. In Joy's own language, each poem, accompanied by a reflection leading into prayer or meditation, grows out of her own struggle to describe the indescribable. This series of poems is inspired by the writer's struggles to reconcile personal experience of Holy Mystery with traditional church doctrine and teaching. Her poems encompass a broad range of theological perspectives and enunciate different images of God.

It is the hope of the poet and this bishop that the poems in this collection will speak to people of all faiths and perhaps to those with no faith at all. Joy MacCormick, a fifth-generation New Zealander, mother, grandmother, priest and poet, invites you to entertain her questions and engage with her journey as she continues to explore and discover new experiences and understandings of God.

I trust you will enjoy the honesty and the beauty of *Moments of Grace*.

The Right Reverend David Rice
Bishop of Waiapu, The Anglican Church in Aotearoa, New Zealand and Polynesia

Introduction

In this 21st century, many people struggle to find relevance in the traditional ways of thinking about God, reflecting, as they do, the experience and worldview of a time and a culture so different from today's. The insights of Carl Gustav Jung and others have provided new ways of understanding humanity and its relationship with the Holy; technology, quantum physics and cosmology extend our perception of God's creative power and activity; ancient wisdom teachings are shown to contain truths far beyond what we have accorded them. Every moment, every experience, offers opportunity for a grace-filled encounter with God. What an exciting time for people of faith!

Pontius Pilate asked Jesus, 'What is truth?' (John 18:38). Perhaps the church needs to ask the same question rather than insisting that what has been received, and the form in which it has been received, is 'the truth, the whole truth, and nothing but the truth'. Biblical scholarship, church history and recent translations of writings from the early years of Christianity suggest that such a claim may be not only arrogant but also patently erroneous. What has been traditionally understood and proclaimed may well be truth but it is not, and cannot be, the whole truth. To insist that it is is to set limits on God's revelation and, indeed, on God's very being. It is to claim that what does not accord with what I already know cannot be of God; that God has nothing more to teach me. The God I have come to know is so much more than this!

This book is, I hope, like a collection of keys to open awareness to the richness, diversity, wonder and mystery we name as 'God'. Meditative verse and related devotional pieces explore the delight, frustration, darkness and light of intimacy and abandonment in relationship with that God. I invite you to enter the sacred space of your own experience of the Holy and to move beyond familiarity into the unknown, daring to explore images and encounters that may be unfamiliar, even uncomfortable or challenging at times. In the course of that exploration, may you feel encouraged to step into a deeper relationship with God, with others and with your own self.

Some suggestions may be helpful, as this book is not designed to be read from beginning to end but, rather, to be mined for hidden treasure.

- For personal prayer or for reading on a time of retreat: Slowly explore the titles or dip into the pages at random until one catches your attention. Read the poem slowly—maybe several times—allowing it to speak into your spirit. Pause to explore, to ponder any word, phrase or concept that invites you to journey deeper. Suggestions on the right-hand page are offered to help your reflection but feel free to set them aside and follow the leading of the Holy Spirit as you contemplate God's word to you.
- For use with groups: For a half-day, one piece should provide plenty of material; this might also be enough for a full day, depending on how much reflection time you allow, or you could combine two (for example, pairing 'Invitation' with something like 'Discovering self'; 'Baptism' with 'Wilderness' or 'God of emptiness and silence'). Related material of your own choosing (music, scripture or other readings, prayer, creative activities and so on) would enhance the event and make it more your own. The process suggested in the previous paragraph may be appropriate to include.

Many people find that keeping a personal, private journal of their experiences in prayer and times of reflection is a way to deepen and enrich their relationship with the Holy. To do this, regularly record both inner events (such as prayer experiences, feelings, questions, dreams) and outer events (special scripture passages that catch your attention, encounters with people that affect you, special films or TV programmes, worship experiences). These can all be clues from God to indicate the next step on your spiritual journey, signs of God's presence in your life at this time. Keeping a record of such things makes it possible to revisit them and ask 'Where was/is God in this? What was/is God showing me in this?'

A key to effective journal writing is 'No JAM': no Judging; no Analysing; no Mucking about. Just let your writing flow: you may be surprised when you look back at what you have written. On a time of retreat I was struggling to integrate the 'Mary/Martha' aspects of myself. On the final day I found that in my journal I had unknowingly written the name 'Marthy'. When I shared this with my spiritual director, he said, 'I'm never going to call you anything else!' He never did until the day he died—and I have never forgotten the lesson or the experience of bringing those two elements of myself together in wholeness.

Meister Eckhart (d. 1329) wrote:

'What is God? God is!
    Creation is the giving of Isness from God.'

May you be richly blessed by many moments of grace as you seek deeper encounter with the One who is.

Exploration and discovery

Paradox

The God I know is paradox!
Is never this or that
But both and neither;
Transcendent source of everything,
yet immanent—close presence;
ineffable—beyond all words and language;
changeless, within an ever-changing revelation;
constant, and yet reshaping and transforming
from what has been to what is yet to be;
giver of life, receiver of the dead;
the source and destiny of all that is;
holding diversity in perfect unity.

Where do I begin?

Deep in my spirit I have always known
that I existed long before
my parents clothed me in humanity.

I came unwilling to this earthly life
from where I was—held close
in perfect love and harmony.

Six years I struggled to escape, return
to what I'd known and thought I'd lost—
a close relationship with God.

It took another forty years to realise
I'd not been 'sent away'
but offered opportunity to share in God's own being—

for

did not God also take human form?

Did each of us 'begin' when born, when conceived, or at some distant unknown time?

In his poem 'Ode: Intimations of Immortality', William Wordsworth wrote:

Our birth is but a sleep and a forgetting:
The Soul that rises with us, our life's Star
Hath had elsewhere its setting,
And cometh from afar:
Not in entire forgetfulness,
And not in utter nakedness,
But trailing clouds of glory do we come
From God, who is our home:
Heaven lies about us in our infancy!

How do you respond to this?

The psalmist also had a sense of pre-existence, long before birth. Read and reflect on Psalm 139, especially verses 13–16.

The unique combination of genetic material that forms my body may have come into being at the moment of conception, yet geneticists can trace its component parts back through countless generations. So when did I begin?

Quantum physics teaches that every particle of energy within the cosmos can be traced back to a single source—the original 'big bang'. The subatomic particles of every atom of my body share that common source. In reality I am formed not only of the dust of the earth but of stardust. So when did I begin?

Allow yourself to wonder at the ways in which scientific discoveries are confirming long-held intuitions about God's creative work reflected in the universe and in your own being.

Heresy?

I heard myself, that morning, speak it out—
a wondering about the purpose of my life;
a wondering about the richness of the past few years
so full of learning, growth, new understandings
of old familiar truths.

All at once the wonderings came together,
and there it was before me.
Could it be that I was put into this life
To share the truths that I am now discovering?
Those truths which sound so deep within
that I cannot deny, cannot resist
the resonance that rises from my inmost being
however strange they seem.

If this, if these, be heresy
then may I have the courage
to wear with grace and pride
the name of heretic.

To many people, the word 'heresy' means anything that differs from received, established, generally accepted truth—especially as taught by those in authority. Yet truth, even about God, is not static. It is constantly evolving as new discoveries are made. Orthodox theology of the 17th century held that the earth was the centre of the universe because it had been visited by God. Galileo was declared heretical for denying this and claiming that the earth orbited the sun. Modern scientific discoveries offer enormous opportunity to expand our awareness of the wonder of the cosmos and of God. Is all such knowledge to be deemed heresy?

Think back over your lifetime. Do you still believe that your parents are or were infallible? What other childhood beliefs or under-standings have changed or been set aside as you have grown?

Are there earlier beliefs or understandings about God that you have set aside or now question? What are they? Are there new concepts that you have accepted or rejected? What and why?

Jesus said, 'The Spirit of truth... will guide you into all the truth... and... will declare to you the things that are to come' (John 16:13). If all truth is already received, what is the need for this? Or is the Spirit no longer a source of revelation of God's truth?

The Greek root of the word 'heresy' (*haeresis*) means 'choice or thing chosen', so heresy means thinking or choosing for oneself rather than depending only on what others say or teach.

Could it be more heretical to cling to old, outdated beliefs and understandings than to be open to new revelation? What is meant by 'Be transformed by the renewing of your minds, so that you may discern what is the will of God—what is good and acceptable and perfect' (Romans 12:2)?

How would you feel if others called you 'heretic'?

Hide and seek

Come! Come!
Come find me where you've never looked before!
Why do you seek me where you've always sought?
Am I not more imaginative than that?

Come! Take a chance, a risk.
Dare to leave the old familiar paths
and wander, eyes and heart wide open,
toward my voice as I call out your name.

Come! Play with me!
Don't be so deadly earnest, so unsmiling.
Relax and learn to play, to laugh aloud.
Become a child again, and learn delight
in seeking what you think you may have lost.

If you would truly know where I am hidden
then give yourself completely to the searching.
Venture where you've never thought to go.
I promise—if you seek me you will find me,
for I will call your name and draw you near.

So much has been made of the need to search diligently for God, to devote the whole of life to this endeavour (Matthew 7:7–8 often being quoted), that it seems all sense of delight in the search has been lost. There is seldom any recognition that God not only participates in the process but actually initiates it. God is the ultimate seeker who never gives up. Yet, like a parent who plays hide-and-seek with a child, when roles are reversed God draws the seeker into new experiences, into previously unexplored territory, but never into any real danger.

The story is told of a young child sharing with Grandma their fear of 'God who's always watching, and waiting to punish me if I do something wrong'. Grandma, with the wisdom of age and experience, replies, 'No. It's not like that. It's just that God can't bear to look away from you—not even for a moment. God loves you so much.'

Many people feel separated from God at some time. Do you believe it is possible to be (not just to feel) apart from God?

'Simply to exist is to be with God and within God,' wrote Meister Eckhart (c.1260–1329), and 'Outside of God there is nothing but nothing.'

Do you believe there is anywhere God cannot be?

If so, where do you believe this is?

Read and reflect on Psalm 139, especially verses 7–12.

In what dark, closed-off or neglected corners of your life might God be hiding and calling for you?

Read and reflect on Psalm 27, especially verses 8–9.

The face of God

If I would recognise the face of God
the blind eyes of my heart need opening
to Holy Presence, not just in human form
but in earth and sea and sky
and all that is.

The story tells that for a few brief years
the face of God was seen in human guise—
but did folk recognise the face
or hear the invitation to God's feast?

If God became what we are—shared our humanity,
that we might share in being what God is—
then every human face, no matter how disfigured,
how distorted, reveals the presence
of the One I name as God.

Not only that—but everything I see or hear,
all that I touch or taste or smell
(whether in delight or with revulsion),
conveys God's presence.

Too briefly have I glimpsed this truth
in moments of deep contemplation;
known perfect unity with all that is—
known perfect unity with God.

From earliest times humans have sensed something in nature that evokes awe. Even those who profess no faith pause to marvel at a sunset, snowcapped mountains against a deep blue sky, the power and ferocity of volcano or earthquake. Today quantum physicists are aware of a 'life force' (for want of a better term) in subatomic particles, which enables them to respond and change when observed. The whole understanding of the universe, its origin and operation, is undergoing a transformation and, though a different language is used, ancient wisdom passed on in faith stories is being confirmed.

For example, the Judeo-Christian story speaks of nothingness until God spoke and all things were created (Genesis 1:1–3). What was the sound of God's first utterance if not a silence-shattering 'big bang'?

Meister Eckhart encourages us to 'become aware of God in every thing, for every single creature is full of God'. He also writes, 'What is God? God is! Creation is the giving of Isness from God.'

Take yourself to some special place where you can relax and be aware of all that surrounds you. (If this is not possible in reality, find a comfortable spot where you will be undisturbed and let your imagination take you to such a place, or just lie down on the grass.)

Using all your senses, become aware of everything surrounding you and of your body as part of the scene. As you take some deep relaxing breaths, feel the energy of life, of God, entering and flowing through every part of your being. See and feel that same energy expressed in everything around you, connecting you to all creation (including every other human being) and to God.

Can you carry this connectedness into your daily life?

Might it change any of your attitudes or actions towards other people or towards planet earth?

Devious God

'God is a perfect gentleman,' I've heard them say.
'Will not intrude, impose, must be invited.'
Excuse me if I dare to disagree!
The God I've learned to recognise
is more bulldozer than invited guest;
comes crashing in at unexpected moments,
destroying, tearing down, demolishing
all I have thought secure.

'God is a crutch the weak depend upon.'
If God's a crutch, a prop, then this is one
crutch I can do without!
The more I know of God, the less I trust
in God's support along the path I choose.
God is no crutch to help me on my way;
more like a captor forcing me
along a path I have no wish to tread.

In the beginning, all they said was true—
I, being wooed with gentlemanly love,
Said 'Come into my heart, my life.'
God came—reordered my priorities; swept out
so many of the things I deeply treasured;
impelled me down a rough and dangerous path
towards the unknown realm of life in all its fullness.
God, offered but an inch, had seized a mile!

Spiritual growth, I believe, is less to do with church involvement than with development into the fullnesss of one's potential. To promote growth, God digs for what is buried deep within, and it is in this context that God as bulldozer is likely to be encountered. While it appears big, clumsy and destructive, a well-driven bulldozer can delicately and precisely remove any part of a structure that is no longer needed or tear up a roadway that has served its purpose and needs to be replaced. This often brings protest, anger, intense resistance and resentment at the intrusion into what is familiar and valued.

God's purpose is never wanton destruction, although, to my limited vision, it often seems so at the time. Once the obstructions have been removed and I have a wider, clearer view, I can move on to explore yet another undiscovered country—a country to which the path of my own choice would not have brought me.

In your relationship with God, who is in control?

How far are you willing or able to trust the God who drives a bulldozer through your life?

Do not remember the former things,
or consider the things of old.
I am about to do a new thing;
now it springs forth, do you not perceive it?
I will make a way in the wilderness
and rivers in the desert.

Isaiah 43:18–19

Discovering self

From the shadows of your fears and dark imaginings
I have called you
to the deeper darkness of the unknown reaches of your being.
I have drawn you by the longing, deep within you.
to discover all that wholeness which I give.

Your joy in finding light where you feared darkness,
discovering the beauty long concealed,
is but a taste of what full life can offer
to those who choose, and dare, to travel
in the land which calls them on.

Go now, assured that in that landscape—
all unmapped, uncharted, in your eyes—
others have travelled and will journey with you.
Fear not to walk with them, and learn, and grow.
For all lies open now and full of promise.
Your pain and fears are fertile soil
for seeds to grow, and flower, and bear much fruit.

According to the Gospel of Luke (9:23–25), self is to be denied, yet simultaneously to be valued above all else. The use of the word 'self' for two different realities has often led to confusion and unhealthy self-denigration.

The self to be denied is the egotistical 'me first' self. The self to be valued is each person's God-given identity—the individual expression of what psychologist Carl Gustav Jung called the *Imago Dei*, the image of God at the core of every human, treasure buried in the depth of one's inmost being.

The darkness so often feared when turning inwards is, according to Jung, 90 per cent pure gold. It is a paradox that the inner journey towards wholeness, while essentially solitary, is shared with many others.

Do you fear any darkness within?

Dare you trust God enough to journey into that darkness?

Jesus said, 'You will know the truth, and the truth will make you free' (John 8:32).

And of him it was written, 'The light shines in the darkness, and the darkness did not overcome it' (John 1:5).

Insight

Hello Fear, my old companion.
It's been a while since you have showed your face—
yet I have sensed you on my pathway;
lurking in the shadows, round the corners.
I thought I'd grown resistant to your dire predictions
but last night, through some crevice in my armour
your arrow, sharp and barbed, found—once again—its mark.
This time, however, I can name the marksman
and so can turn and meet you face to face.
How small you are when looked upon directly.
How weak you have become since last we met;
your size and power but shadow and illusion.

Take back your arrow, Fear, and leave my presence!
I choose to travel on with Trust and Love.

Fear is a powerful emotion: it is essential for protection from danger and preservation of life, but it can also cripple and immobilise. Like anger, it is neither good nor bad in itself, but unawareness of its presence and its power can be disastrous.

People driven by fear become defensive and, like cornered animals, likely to strike out at any perceived threat. Such fear, usually unrecognised and unnamed, underlies most forms of extremism.

Recognising fear brings the opportunity to consider what it is that feels threatened and why. Sometimes what is feared is the invitation to a deeper relationship, new understandings, fuller life or greater wholeness. Such invitations to leave behind what is familiar and journey into unknown territory are not always welcome.

When fears are named, their power is diminished and it becomes possible to choose one's response. Big fears tend to be easily recognised and the choice of flight or fight is often clear. The multitude of little unnamed fears are subtler in the ways they sabotage fullness of life.

How much of your life is controlled by fear?

What lurks beneath the 'shoulds' and 'don'ts' that control your behaviour and your choices?

Prayerfully make a list of all the fears you can name—big and small. Are there any that surprise you?

Read and reflect on Psalm 91, taking each of the threats as a metaphor for inner struggles.

'Perfect love casts out fear' (1 John 4:18). How do you now understand this verse?

Contemplation

Whenever I fail
to notice what I notice,
filling my days instead
with unawareness,

I miss so many
'transient rainbow things'; [1]
so many 'passing instants'
which cannot be regained.

Pausing to become aware,
to wonder at
the gift of life,
the beauty of creation,

I find again
the point of equilibrium,
and in the transient rainbow
of the passing instant

   I rejoice.

So much of the world today focuses on productivity, placing high value on what is instant and disposable. The pace of life becomes ever more frenetic and stressful, dominated by clocks inexorably marking off hours, minutes, even seconds.

Do you yearn for a more relaxed, more gentle way of being; for time to watch the clouds drift by, listen to birdsong or linger over the beauty of a flower without a sense of guilt over 'wasting time'?

Once long, long ago—before humans captured time and imprisoned it in clocks—life was attuned to the rhythms of nature, the ebb and flow of tides and seasons.

When did you last step aside from busyness:

To see the world in a grain of sand
And heaven in a wild flower,
Hold infinity in the palm of your hand
And eternity in an hour? [2]

An hour, or even a few moments, can be enough to reconnect with the source of all that is, to nourish the spirit, to lift the heart in rejoicing.

Take a few moments to feed your soul. Set aside some regular 'transient rainbow moments'. Young children are great teachers in finding moments of awe and wonder. Is that why Jesus said, 'Unless you change and become like children, you will never enter the kingdom of heaven' (Matthew 18:3)?

YHWH

God.
Creating, unifying,
more verb than noun;
moving towards fulfilment
all that is.

God.
Essence of life,
wild cosmic energy,
sustaining, ever changing,
ever constant.

God.
Known yet unknown,
transcending definition;
within whom I live and move
and have my being.

God.
Three-letter word;
so small yet signifying
more than the human mind
can comprehend.

YHWH—the unpronounceable name of holy mystery, beyond definition yet rooted in the verb 'to be': 'God said to Moses, "I AM WHO I AM"' (Exodus 3:14).

When the word 'God' is used, there is usually an assumption that all who hear will know what is being talked about. The reality is that each person's concept of God may be very different.

According to Richard Rohr (Fransiscan priest, author and international speaker), the word YHWH is a breathed prayer—requiring no shaping by lips, tongue or voice. References to God as breath or wind are found throughout the Bible, from creation (Genesis 1:2) to Pentecost (Acts 2:2), and carry a sense of ever-moving power that is not static and cannot be limited or directed by human action.

Find yourself a quiet space and centre your heart and mind on God—whatever that word means to you. Relax and steady your breathing. Be aware of God's presence in every breath you take. With lips slightly parted, draw in God's Spirit. Without moving lips or tongue, gently breathe out the sound 'Yah'. Draw in your next breath with the sound 'weh'—again without moving lips or tongue. Repeat until the action feels natural, and let yourself be filled with the divine presence beyond all naming. Journal your experience.

Meister Eckhart said, 'I pray God to rid me of God.' How do you respond to this?

Struggle

Desolation

When dreams dissolve and hope proves hollow;
when the centre crumbles as foundations fail;
when ache of emptiness engulfs and overwhelms;
when sorrow seeps into the marrow of my being ...

Heart-crushed by grief, I scarce can breathe,
and numbness is the only thing I feel.
Paralysis prevails, all energy is gone;
so, too, desire to ever move again.

Then, Dark Despair, I know you wait
to call me to your realm of endless night.
How easy now to sink and sleep submerged
beneath the waters of oblivion.

But there are those who need me here,
battered and bloodied though I be.
For them I will endure this agony—
and seek to live again.

Like earthquake or avalanche, pain and despair burst unexpectedly into human lives, threatening to overwhelm or destroy. Inability to change or control events, to predict their duration or the outcome, intensifies suffering. God seems utterly remote or absent and, seeking to escape the pain, even death can seem an attractive option.

Yet some part of me knows, beyond all doubt, that I am not abandoned by the One who promises to be present through fire and flood (Isaiah 43:2), and I turn again to Psalm 46:1–2, 7 for encouragement.

> *God is our refuge and strength, a very present help in trouble.*
> *Therefore we will not fear, though the earth should change,*
> *though the mountains shake in the heart of the sea...*
> *The Lord of hosts is with us; the God of Jacob is our refuge.*

Either physically or in imagination, take yourself to a place that feels safe (maybe a favourite chair, the shelter of a special tree, the company of someone who holds and protects you or a garden corner). Settle into it and then reflect on these questions:

- What have been the most difficult times in your life? Times when you have found it hard to trust or even to believe in God?
- What sustained you and led you through those times?
- With the wisdom of hindsight, what gifts of learning or growth did you receive?
- Can life in all its fullness be known without experience of the depths?

> *Jesus, Saviour in storm,*
> *when the waters of the deep are broken up,*
> *when the landmarks are washed away or drowned,*
> *come to us across the water.*

COLLECT FOR EPIPHANY 6, *A NEW ZEALAND PRAYER BOOK* (HE *KARAKIA MIHINARE O AOTEAROA*), P. 568

God of emptiness and silence

If what I now experience of God
is quite unlike all I have known before,
have I been self-deceived, or been betrayed?

That strong yet gentle, all-embracing presence
now only absence, emptiness and silence;
delight replaced by pain, and song by lamentation.

Has God abandoned me and left me desolate?
Or could it be that, trusting in my love,
God dares reveal a less attractive face—
hoping that I'll not turn away, rejecting?

If God is also emptiness and silence
as I've, in awe, been drawn to contemplate—
then, this deep aching void may offer evidence
of moving closer to the God I love.

In what I thought was absence, I know presence.
With emptiness I can begin to fill.
In silence, know the word of life is spoken
and learn, with Love's own voice, to resonate.

Reluctance to let go of familiar, comfortable images is a sure sign of stagnation in my relationship with God. It is to insist that God conform to my expectations and to deny that God might be anything more, anything other than my definition.

When all images are stripped away; when God is experienced as emptiness and silence; when all prayer and weeping seem to go unheard; when the sense of abandonment threatens to overwhelm—then I have entered that dark, unbounded desert place and must choose whether to turn back in fear or to journey on in growing trust and love.

Maybe, when I feel most abandoned it is the time when I am closest to the one who cried from the cross, 'My God, my God, why have you forsaken me?' (Matthew 27:46).

Read and reflect on the following passages.

How long, O Lord? Will you forget me for ever?
How long will you hide your face from me?
How long must I bear pain in my soul,
and have sorrow in my heart all day long?
But I trusted in your steadfast love;
my heart shall rejoice in your salvation.

PSALM 13:1–2, 5

O my God, I cry by day, but you do not answer;
and by night, but find no rest…
On you I was cast from my birth,
and since my mother bore me you have been my God…
I will tell of your name to my brothers and sisters;
in the midst of the congregation I will praise you.

PSALM 22:2, 10, 22

What is your preferred image of God? Why?

Is it time for you to let go of it?

What might happen if you do?

Rough play

Capricious God!
Your play can be so gentle or so rough.
Sometimes it hardly seems like play at all
but more like wanton teasing.
Like cat with mouse you bat me to and fro;
you toss me up and catch me;
you let me run, then pounce on me again.
There's no escape.

I feel so bruised and battered, God, today;
the victim of harsh bullying abuse.
And yet you ask me, once again, to trust you.
You ask a lot! But then you always do.
All that I have and am; all that I shall become.
There's part of me would turn away and flee
from this demand.

When pain would overwhelm, may I remember
Job knew both good and evil at your hand;
the psalmist recognised there's no escaping;
and Peter understood you as the source of life.
So may I trust that one day I will know again
your other face of constancy and love.

Help me hold on to that!

My relationship with God is not all gentleness and light. Like any love relationship, it is tempered by times of bewilderment, pain and anger—precipitated by God's apparent lack of care. At these times, pretending all is well is an attempt to deceive both myself and God.

In such a situation it can be helpful to recall the ancient Jewish teaching that God dispenses blessings from both hands. From the right hand flow the blessings we enjoy; from the left, those blessings we often fail to recognise and struggle to accept.

In the book of Job we read of God, in a wager with Satan, allowing his faithful servant to be stripped of all that he had—wealth, family and health. Yet Job refused to curse God and continued to trust.

Read and reflect on these verses.

> *'Shall we receive the good at the hand of God, and not receive the bad?'*
> JOB 2:10

> *'Lord, to whom can we go? You have the words of eternal life.'*
> JOHN 6:68

How honest are you with God about your feelings?

What are you reluctant to share? Why?

Try to share it now—and wait for God's response.

Journal your experience.

Bossy God

Bossy God!
Can you not let me be?
Not for a little while?
It seems the answer's 'No!'

Just when my life seems settled
you call me on again.
Maybe it's time I learned
the absolute futility of all resistance.
You will have your way
in spite of my reluctance.

Deep in my heart I know
your way will bring
peace, freedom,
and a closer walk with you.

Anger is a powerful source of energy but is not necessarily sin. It is, in fact, one of the attributes of God. Scriptural references to God's anger abound: just check any concordance. The Gospels also record Jesus being angry about injustice and lack of integrity—as well as that episode in the temple (Mark 11:15–19).

The potential for sin lies not in anger itself but in how we deal with it. When denied and repressed, anger festers in the subconscious, eventually erupting uncontrollably and destructively. Conscious acknowledgment of our anger empowers choice about how best to use its energy constructively or defuse it safely—perhaps by letting God deal with it.

Scripture says, 'Be angry but do not sin; do not let the sun go down on your anger' (Ephesians 4:26). If anger is not recognised and named, how can sin be avoided?

I was angry with my friend;
I told my wrath, my wrath did end.
I was angry with my foe;
I told it not, my wrath did grow.[3]

How honest are you with yourself about what angers you?

How honest are you willing or able to be with God?

Invite God to walk with you through memories of your anger. If you were to trust God with your anger, what might that do for God?

Homecoming

For many months I wandered in a dry and dreary land;
a place of stones and quite devoid of growth.
Each month seemed a year, so long it took to pass,
yet all the while I knew I wandered there by my own choice.

I did not choose that it should be so lonely,
so silent, barren, colourless and cold.
I chose it to escape from what it seemed Love beckoned me to do,
and running from Love's voice, I ran from Love's own self.

Love, knowing all my fear, still called to me
and waited patiently for me to turn again;
to recognise my home, my rightful place.

Daring, at last, to face the dreaded darkness,
I saw the shadows melt, evaporate, dissolve.
A road stretched out, divided in the distance,
and where it forked there stood a house I recognised.
A candle burned inside an upper window—
a beacon, lit by Love, to draw me back.

The door stood open and I ran.
Then, on Love's lap I wept for all the loss and pain
My fear and selfishness had caused.
Love held me close as tears ran down my face,
And when, in choking voice, I sobbed,
'I really do love you', Love smiled.
'There's only one of us,' Love said,
'who ever doubted that.'

In any love relationship there comes a time when the call to total commitment can no longer be ignored. Some inner wisdom knows that both joy and pain are hidden in the invitation, for, whatever the answer, some sacrifice will be inevitable. Sometimes the cost of choosing seems so high, it outweighs any possibility of benefit or gain. Yet the choice is always ours and must be made—even deciding not to choose is a choice—and each one must live with the consequences of the decision. The good news is that, in God's love, any choice offers opportunity for redemption, growth and healing.

Augustine of Hippo wrote, 'You have made us for yourself, O Lord, and our hearts are restless until they rest in you' (*Confessions*, Book 1 Chapter 1).

Have you known this restlessness? When? Why?

Has it been resolved? What brought this resolution about?

If unresolved, what is needed for you to find rest?

Jesus told a story of a son who rejected his father's love, and a father who never stopped loving—even in the face of that rejection. Slowly read Luke 15:11–32, several times. Be aware of anything that catches your attention and write it down so that you can return to it. Why might this particular word or idea be speaking to you right now? Hold it in prayer in the presence of Love and journal what you experience.

Born again

Why do they speak of 'being born again'
   as if it were an 'only once' event
   and easy, full of joy?

It seems I've known, so many times,
   a birth into new life.
   Not once has it been easy!
      Joy comes only when the birth is over.

The God who gave, who gives me life,
   calls me repeatedly to travel
   the birth canal of pain towards a new creation;
      to leave behind the safe, familiar place
         in which I've lived and moved and had my being
            and face once more the separation and the letting
            go—
               for new life I can find no other way.

This birthing can't be rushed.
   While being born, I'm called to bring to birth
   the life of God within me.
      No wonder that the pain is so intense!

There is no turning back, no respite.
   Labour must proceed until new life appears.
   God, give me grace to know you in the birth pangs.

Jesus tells Nicodemus that he must be born again (John 3:1–10), calling him into newness of life through the experience of a spiritual rebirth. Nicodemus, as a leader of his people, was secure in his knowledge and understanding of God, yet open enough to approach Jesus whose proclamation offered something different—open enough to accept the challenge to learn more (v. 10).

Before birth, a child knows deep intimacy with its mother, yet that form of intimacy must be broken as the child is thrust forth into the world. It is only through expulsion from the safe haven of the womb into a new and different way of being, through learning to be apart, to endure separation, that the relationship can grow. The child must accept the pain of apparent rejection in order to see its mother face-to-face and discover the fullness of life and love—and this is only the first of many such losses, which usher in new life.

How is this picture reflected in relationship with God?

Is it possible to become too comfortable with God? Does a close relationship run the risk of complacency or even stagnation? What are the dangers of thinking we know all there is to be known of God?

Have you known, or do you now know, God as midwife—ushering in new life through the pain of separation?

It has been said that the role of the church is 'to comfort the disturbed and to disturb the comfortable'. Do you agree with this? Why or why not?

Journal a conversation with God about this.

Surrender

For long and weary weeks, months, years,
the journey led through bleak and barren landscape
where all my praying, seeking,
all pleading, weeping, raging,
were swallowed in the silence of the void
from which no whispered echo was returned.

Yet even in that place of desolation—
in spite of everything that would deny it—
somehow conviction that God is remained.
No more than that.
Who, what or where God is
all stripped away—
and in despairing agony I grieved.

Deeper and deeper still into the void
some power drew me on.
I sought, but lacked, the energy to stop
until, spent and exhausted,
all striving and resistance broken,
I surrendered
and
f
  e
    l
     l
            into the very heart of God.

Meister Eckhart said that whatever one believes God to be is not actually God. How do you respond to this?

Have you ever experienced, or are you now experiencing, a sense of being abandoned by the God you have known?

If so, know that you are not alone, that this is an intrinsic part of the journey to a deeper relationship and that it is well documented by others who have travelled in that land. However it is named—desert time, absence of God, the void, the dark night of the soul or (as an anonymous medieval writer called it) the 'cloud of unknowing' (that place where all that is known becomes unknown)—this time of indescribable loneliness and doubt is a crucible from which faith, tested to its limit, emerges triumphant and transformed. What has been stripped away is replaced by unimagined, often indescribable richness and a certainty that the God of 'deep and dazzling darkness' (Henry Vaughan, 1621–1695) has been a presence in the absence.

Are you willing to let go of all you know of God in order to find more of God?

Can you trust in God's love—no matter what?

Read Psalms 42 and 43 and reflect on the writer's experience. How does it speak into your own?

Hear the cry of the psalmist: 'I say to God, my rock, "Why have you forgotten me?"' (Psalm 42:9). Feel God's presence with you in your abandonment.

Celebration

Invitation

Come, join the dance of life.
Let music fasten wings on your soul's feet
to loose you from their heavy measured tread—
that you might move in freedom and with grace.

Allow rainbows to wrap you
in a cloak of celebration,
that you may shed the tattered careworn rags
so tightly clutched about you.

Unlock the shackles
binding you to rules and regulations.
Feel the bright new music resonate within.
Come, join the dance of life.

Does your spirit yearn for freedom, for life in all its fullness?

What holds you back from this?

What voices say, 'You shouldn't...'?

What rules are you afraid to break?

Who made these rules?

Jesus said, 'I came that they may have life, and have it abundantly' (John 10:10) and disregarded the rules of his culture and religious tradition where he saw that they restricted life and freedom. He also had harsh words for those who sought to impose such constraints on others: 'They tie up heavy burdens, hard to bear, and lay them on the shoulders of others, but they themselves are unwilling to lift a finger to move them' (Matthew 23:4).

Think back over your life to the time you felt most free and most fully yourself. Let yourself relive that experience and dwell in the delight of it.

Do you recognise it as a gift from God?

What have you done with this gift? Where is it now?

Talk with God about what you will do with your one precious life. Journal your conversation.

God's loving

I called you into being.
I fashioned you, unseen, into my likeness.
I planted, deep within you, my own spirit.
How, then, could I not love you as you are?

What you reject,
despise and criticise in others,
reflects what you deny about yourself,
fearing that even I cannot accept it.

I do not seek perfection—
but willingness to grow; to share my love;
to be a clear reflection, an image of my presence.
Go now—and be my window for the world.

'You shall love... your neighbour as yourself' (Luke 10:27).

It has been said, 'When you see how most Christians love themselves, it's no wonder their neighbours get such a raw deal' and 'What you find unacceptable in yourself you will be unable to accept in another.' Is it because we find it almost impossible to love ourselves, 'warts and all', that we find it so hard to believe that God can do so?

Has the call to 'Be perfect' (Matthew 5:48) contributed to a sense of inevitable failure to measure up to God's expectations, to be acceptable to God? Is this one root of the deep split in the human psyche that leads us either to see ourselves as 'miserable sinners', constantly unworthy of love, or so to repress any sense of our own sin that we project it all on to 'those terrible others'— feeling more acceptable in comparison with them?

What difference does it make to know that the Greek word *teleios*, translated in Matthew 5:48 as 'perfect', carries, as one of its root meanings, the sense of 'being in the process of becoming' or 'moving towards fulfilment of purpose' rather than of having arrived at some predetermined state?

Recognising that we share imperfection with all humanity, that we all 'sin' or fall short of the mark (Romans 3:23, a term taken from archery), opens us to the possibility of growth towards the fulfilment of God's purpose for each one of us and enables greater transparency in our dealings with each other and with God.

Try praying the Agnus Dei, varying its meaning by emphasising different words. For example:

Lamb of God, you take away the sin of the world;
have mercy on us.
Lamb of God, you take away the sin of the world,
have mercy on us.
Lamb of God, you take away the sin of the world,
grant us your peace.

Magnificat

From deep within the centre of my being
a wordless song of praise begins to rise.
On silent wings it soars
to meet the deeper silence whence it came.
No word is needed.
No sound dare I utter.
Lest, all discordant, it disrupt this harmony
touching transcendence.

So silence calls to silence
and all eternity re-echoes with the song.

While the experience of transcendence can come upon us unexpectedly, most of us only enter that realm when we make a conscious choice to draw aside from the frenetic pace of daily life.

Opportunities to 'take time out with God' may be few and far between, like going on a retreat, or they may be briefer and more frequent times of contemplation. Like precious jewels scattered through the sands of life, they're there for us to find—if we but make the effort.

In his poem 'God's grandeur', Gerard Manley Hopkins writes, 'The world is charged with the grandeur of God.' In my beautiful homeland of Aotearoa/New Zealand, I am surrounded with evidence of God's presence in mountain, bush, lake and ocean, in sunshine and in abundance of water.

When did you last take time to notice God's grandeur all around you?

Take time to become aware of it now or visit and spend time in an environment that is special to you.

What causes your heart to soar in thanksgiving?

Mary responded to God in a song of thanksgiving that we know as the Magnificat (Luke 1:46–55). Try writing your own Magnificat.

The thrush

Outside the window of my hermitage,
low in the ginko tree,
a thrush has built her nest.

Last week she sat on eggs;
today she nurtures hatchlings—
tiny, blind and helpless.

To feed her chicks she leaves the nest;
deprives them of her warm, protective presence,
exposing them to sun and wind and rain.

Instinctively she knows this must be so.
To grow, her young will need not only food
but space to spread their wings.

They need the freedom to lift up their heads
and look beyond the safety of the nest—
until, one day, they have the strength to fly.

Her absences grow longer day by day.
She watches from ever greater distance.
Yet, always, she returns to meet their need.

One day her young will fledge, will leave the nest,
will seek for independence and for freedom.
For this she gave them life. For this she reared them.

The image of God as a mother bird—warm, protective and nurturing—is both attractive and scriptural ('As an eagle stirs up its nest, and hovers over its young... the Lord alone guided him', Deuteronomy 32:11–12; 'How often have I desired to gather your children together as a hen gathers her brood under her wings', Matthew 23:37).

Just as there comes a time when chicks must learn to fly, to find their own nourishment and survive the storms without the presence and protection they have known, so it has been in my relationship with God.

In the beginning, all was tenderness and provision—and I was happy in my immaturity. Then God, like the mother thrush, began to leave me exposed and vulnerable. In spite of my fear of abandonment, there remained, in the depths of my being, an indefinable sense of 'a presence in the absence'. On each occasion, I have learned and grown.

Can you name times when you have felt deserted by God?

What have you learned through these times?

Jesus said, 'It is to your advantage that I go away' (John 16:7). What do you think he meant by this?

The thrush rears her chicks for the freedom essential for them to know fullness of life. Might God will for us the same growth away from infantile dependence?

Winter

Short days, and bleak.
As if, conserving strength,
the sun withdraws into itself
the warmth and light it shared.

Orchard trees lift naked arms
against a slate grey sky.
The energy of all things
spirals inwards to the central core
and all seems dead.

My inner seasons are not
matched to Nature's cycle;
their winter can occur at any time.
My heart needs to remember
that unseen within the sacred dark
energy, turned inward, sparks new life.

Whether it is an inner or an outer event, the season of winter brings both challenge and gift.

When nature's winter storms bring darker, shorter days, bitter winds and ice or snow, it is easy to allow ourselves to become miserable and depressed. We so often forget the gift of time for gathering around fires and snuggling down with bowls of soup, for opportunities to attend to handiwork or reading long set aside, for deeper conversations with family or friends.

When inner life is chilled by loss or pain; when unexpected events bring confusion, darkness or despair; when even the warmth of God's presence and love seems to be withdrawn and all seems frozen—then we need to remember that darkness and chaos are the conditions in which creation originates. 'In the beginning when God created the heavens and the earth, the earth was a formless void and darkness covered the face of the deep, while a wind from God swept over the face of the waters' (Genesis 1:1–2).

Within the bare and apparently lifeless branches of fruit trees, the buds that will produce next season's crop are forming; hidden in the darkness of the soil, seeds germinate; it is in the darkness of the womb that all human life takes shape— and it may be that, in the darkness of my inner winter, new understandings of myself and my relationship with God and others are gestating. They must be allowed to grow unhurried and undisturbed. The 'winter' time is full of potential life and is an essential experience if that life is to develop and come to birth. It was from the cold darkness of the tomb that resurrection life sprang forth (Mark 15:46—16:6).

Look back over the 'winter' seasons of your life.

In those times, what hidden gifts lay buried? How have they grown to produce unexpected fruit?

Offer a prayer of thanksgiving.

When birds no longer flee

When birds no longer flee at my approach,
but turn to look,
then carry on about their own affairs;
when rabbits, in their grazing, merely pause,
and then resume—sensing no threat or danger—
then, then I know I've shed the cloak
of busyness, unfocused energy,
and have come home—
home to deep tranquillity.

I know and love this gentle inner space.
I long to dwell here.
But I am called once more to journey on
into the known yet unknown
mystery of God.

We live in a culture dominated by the passage of hands across the face of a clock; days marked off in calendars and in diaries. We are driven to fill every moment with productivity lest we be accused of wasting time. Like ships ploughing through the ocean, we plough through life setting up great bow waves of energy, disturbing everything in our path and leaving it tossing in our wake.

We forget that long before humans captured time and imprisoned it in clocks, people were aware of a different rhythm— the rhythm of the breath of the universe, the rhythm of life itself.

If and when we choose to step aside from our busyness, intensity and distractions, we can discover ourselves in harmony with all creation—no longer a threat to all that lives. If we open ourselves to the rhythm of God's Spirit breathing into us and through us, we may find ourselves in that 'peaceable kingdom' of which Isaiah writes (11:6–9). Elijah also experienced God's presence in stillness, in 'a sound of sheer silence' rather than in the activity and power of wind, earthquake or fire (1 Kings 19:9–12). Such times can also be moments of awe and fear of what might be asked of us.

Take some time to read and reflect on the above passages or on the words of J.G. Whittier, from his hymn 'Dear Lord and Father of mankind' (1872):

Drop thy still dews of quietness
Till all our strivings cease.
Take from our souls the strain and stress,
And let our ordered lives confess
The beauty of thy peace.

Can you remember a time when you knew this peace and stillness? Do you know it now? How might you encourage its growth in your life?

Approaching storm

Something unknown,
   something disturbing, fills the air—
   hovers just beyond my consciousness.
A change of pressure, a shift of light,
   suggest the calm I now enjoy
   will not, for long, prevail.

The birds have stopped their singing.
Though yet unseen, I sense the dark clouds massing.
The wind begins to gather strength.
The sun's warmth chills.

I shiver—knowing that the storm's about to break—
   and turn to seek for shelter from its wrath.

Storms are not only exterior, meteorological happenings.

Destructive as stormy weather events can be, I find that the storms of my inner life have even greater power to crush and devastate. The chaos I experience in the darkness, the sense of helplessness, my fear of my own fear, can seem quite overwhelming. My initial response is to run before the approaching storm.

Such action, of course, is futile. The brewing storm *will* break —and I will fare much better if I am prepared, if I know where shelter is to be found and gather what resources I may need to see me through.

When, in your life, have you known the approach of a storm? (Perhaps it was the premonition of a disturbance to the pattern of your life, the possibility of diagnosis of a serious illness, a shift in employment or career path or a disturbing dream that haunted your waking hours.)

Have you tried to flee or have you taken time to prepare for what lies ahead? If so, what preparation has proved most beneficial?

What have you learned to help you through future events?

Reflect on these words:

> *Be merciful to me, O God, be merciful to me,*
> *for in you my soul takes refuge.*
> *in the shadow of your wings I will take refuge,*
> *until the destroying storms pass by.*
> *I cry to God Most High,*
> *to God who fulfils his purpose for me.*
>
> PSALM 57:1–2

Long Bay [4]

The waves roll in and wash against the shore
as they have done since time itself began.
Gently caressing, whispering,
they speak of love.

Another day all gentleness is gone—
majestic in power, they pound and pulverise,
demanding nothing less
than full submission.

How like the God I've known!

What seemed capricious, lacking all consideration,
so hurtful at the time,
I now can recognise, and yes,
appreciate as growth-promoting love—
reshaping what had been
to what might be.

This shore, where ocean meets the land,
reflects the meeting of eternity with time.
Liminal space, where spirit meets with matter—
permeating, intermingling.
Evidence that holiness pervades the whole creation
in which we live and move and have our being.

This is the God I know!

As the ocean caresses and reshapes the land, so the Holy Spirit works on our humanity. Openness to change allows reshaping to be as constant and as gentle as the movement of sand on the shore. Where beliefs and attitudes are fixed and rigid, that same reshaping can be experienced as catastrophic and destructive, its creative potential revealed only in later reflection.

Find a comfortable place and relax with a few deep breaths. In imagination, spend some time beside moving water—sea, lake, river or whatever comes to mind. Listen to the sound of the water; watch the play of light on its surface; notice the interaction with the land. How do you feel?

Let the scene change to a stormy day—pounding waves, river in full flood. What sounds do you hear? What changes in the interaction of water and land? How do you now feel? Let the scene fade.

Identify occasions when your life has been like each of these. Where do you now see God at work in them?

Offer a prayer of thanksgiving.

The voice of the Lord is over the waters...
The voice of the Lord is powerful...
The Lord breaks the cedars of Lebanon...
The voice of the Lord flashes forth flames of fire.
The voice of the Lord shakes the wilderness...
The voice of the Lord causes the oaks to whirl,
and strips the forest bare.
PSALM 29:3, 4, 5, 7, 9

The Lord will fulfil his purpose for me;
your steadfast love, O Lord, endures for ever.
PSALM 138:8

'It is the spirit that gives life... The words that I have spoken to
you are spirit and life.'
JOHN 6:63

Gospel moments

Christmastide

Now, once again, you celebrate my birth;
  in pageants re-enact the story;
  sing joyously familiar songs;
    share hospitality.

All this is good—and yet…
  you celebrate a baby in a stable,
  remote in time, non-threatening, and sweet.
    You fail to recognise the deeper mythic truth
      I hoped that you would see.

In every newborn babe I come
  to share again, with all humanity,
  the poverty and illness; pain and persecution;
    the fear of loneliness; rejection by my friends;
      the twisting of my words for evil purpose;
        the crucifixion envious hatred brings.

In every human life I celebrate
  the opening to love, to possibility;
  the courage to explore beyond the boundaries
    of doubt and ignorance—destroyers of the truth;
      each faltering step towards a fuller life.

I have been born in you! Do not deny it!
  In you I seek to walk the earth once more.
  Why do you keep me wrapped in swaddling bands?
    … or are they grave clothes?

Apart from providing a reason for an annual festival of celebration, what relevance does the tale of a birth so long ago in Bethlehem have for 21st-century humankind? How does it address life today?

The story of the incarnation is the story of God (who is spirit) becoming embodied in flesh—of the holy becoming human, thus making all humanity holy. Saint Athanasius (c.296–373) said, 'He became what we are, so that we might become what he is.'

In Jesus we see what life in all its fullness looks like and are challenged to live our own lives according to the model he presents—fully human and fully open to the empowering Holy Spirit of God. We are called, like him, to embody God's presence on earth; like him, to welcome and embrace those whom society (including, too often, the church) excludes; like him, to proclaim the good news of a God of love, forgiveness and healing; like him, to live a countercultural lifestyle—replacing consumerism, exploitation and abuse of creation with justice and equity; like him, to exercise the ministry of reconciliation that Paul declares has been given to us (2 Corinthians 5:18).

This, surely, is the message and the challenge of Christmas—to recognise that to be human means to be holy and to live as a Christ-presence in the world today.

'Christ has no body, now, on earth but yours' (prayer of St Teresa of Avila). Do you believe this? How does it challenge the way you live?

Are you able to recognise, acknowledge and celebrate times when you have been the presence of Christ in some situation? Give thanks for such moments.

Is there anything that prevents you from being a Christ-presence to those whom you meet? Ask God to heal it and set you free to be fully human, fully holy.

Baptism

What drew you to those waters of repentance?
You who, so they tell us, never sinned?
What inner voice, what knowing,
said repentance must precede whatever lay ahead?
What were your hopes, your fears,
your dreams, your expectations,
as you came?

Rising from the waters as one newborn,
you saw the veil of heaven rent violently apart.
Knowing that none could see the face of God and live,
what fear, what terror, flooded through your heart?
Did you expect to die?[5]

Instead of condemnation and destruction
A gentle dove descended, rested on you;
You heard that voice, those words—
'Know this, my child, you are profoundly loved.'

Did the security of love—so deep, so unconditional—
give you courage to proclaim a different God?
If we dared believe that we were loved like this
might we, too, live on earth
as images of God?

According to Mark, the earliest of the Gospel writers:

> *Jesus came... and was baptised by John in the Jordan. And just as he was coming up out of the water, he saw the heavens torn apart and the Spirit descending like a dove on him. And a voice came from heaven, 'You are my Son, the Beloved; with you I am well pleased.'* (Mark 1:9–11)

The Greek word used here for 'torn apart' is also used when, at the time of the crucifixion, 'the curtain of the temple was torn in two, from top to bottom' (Mark 15:38). This word is *schizo*, which carries the sense of being torn with violence.

The gentleness of the descending dove is in strong contrast to the violence that preceded its appearance; both are manifestations of God. There is an ancient Jewish teaching that God prays, 'May it always be my will that my mercy overcome my wrath and that my compassion outweigh my other attributes.'

A gentle God is less familiar to many people than a God of judgment, yet Jesus constantly proclaims a God of forgiveness who seeks to comfort little children—a God of compassion. (The root of the Hebrew word for 'compassion' is the same as that for 'womb'—hence a God of 'womb-love'.) Why is it so difficult to believe in this gentle God? Is such an idea just too good to be true?

Jesus discovered his identity as 'child of God'. How well do I know mine?

It has been said that each one becomes like the God they worship. What kind of God is incarnate in me?

Wilderness

To say, wholeheartedly, a 'yes' to God;
a 'yes' with no provisos, no conditions;
a 'yes' that dares to trust—no matter what may come—
is dangerous!

Such sheer audacity (or foolishness?) invites a challenge,
a test of strength, a probing of its depth.
It was no accident you found yourself,
plunged into barren loneliness
where all was questioned.

When I have found myself adrift, bewildered
in some wilderness that seems to be unending,
how easily I let my fears and doubts develop,
and threaten all I thought I knew.
Bereft of comfort, face to face with all I would avoid,
I struggle to believe this emptiness might be
the place of deeper meeting.

I seldom recognise what brought me here;
what force impelled me from my place of safety,
till looking back, reflecting on the struggle,
I find the anchor of my 'yes' has held.
I know I am indeed profoundly loved.
There is a purpose for my life
that Love will see fulfilled.

*The Spirit immediately drove him out into the wilderness. He was
in the wilderness for forty days, tempted by Satan; and he was
with the wild beasts; and the angels waited on him.*

Mark 1:12–13

In this account by Mark (generally accepted as the earliest of
the four canonical Gospels), Jesus has no time to bask in the
knowledge that he is God's beloved. There is an urgency and
intensity about the transition from baptismal experience to
wilderness: 'the Spirit *immediately drove him out*'. Unlike the
later writers Matthew and Luke, Mark gives no details about the
tests that Jesus faced there, stating only that he was with the
wild beasts.

Was this a geographical wilderness—or was it a place of inner
struggle where questions, doubts and fears rose up like wild
beasts, challenging and threatening to destroy his newfound
sense of identity and purpose as child of God? In either case,
it was a time to become aware of anything that might distract
from, or prevent, response to God's purpose; time to recognise,
name and face it—and, in so doing, to disempower it.

Throughout this testing time, we are told, 'the angels waited
on him'. He was aware, even in the darkest moments, of God's
presence and provision. He was given the courage and strength
needed, not only in that time but for all that lay ahead. It was a
time of discovering just how far he could depend on God and
of daring to move deeper into a relationship of trust and love.

What have been the times and experiences that have best prepared
and equipped you for ministry to others?

What were the issues, the 'wild beasts', with which you struggled
or which tested your faith in God?

What 'angels' sustained you through these times?

Offer a prayer of thanksgiving for learning and growth.

Follow me

What does it mean,
    this call to follow Jesus;
    to leave behind all that
    makes life familiar, comfortable?

Surely it asks for
    more than imitation;
    than mimicking another;
    rejecting who I am.

Jesus lived a life
    uniquely his,
    true to himself
    and what he knew of God.

Might it be possible
    that each is called
    to live into the
    fullness of humanity;

to seek the freedom
    to become what
    they alone can be;
    to be, unique, like Jesus?

Because parts of the church have tended to stress the divinity of Jesus at the expense of his humanity, for many people the call to 'follow Jesus' or to 'be like Jesus' has been understood as an unrealistic call to become what they are not and never can be.

More realistic, and a greater challenge, is to accept that Jesus was indeed 'fully human', that he came (as has been said) not to show us how to be holy but how to be human. If Jesus was fully human, with nothing available to him that is not available to every human being (namely the Holy Spirit of God), then we can no longer claim that it is impossible to live as he did—as fully open to God and to all people; so self-aware that we can act without self-consciousness; so secure in the knowledge of God's love that we can act with absolute integrity even, or especially, in the face of criticism or threat.

'The direct result of exalting Jesus out of his humanity is the development of a faith which is in itself inhuman.'[6] How do you understand this quotation? Do you agree? Why or why not?

What if God's call is actually to grow into all that we have the potential to become; to reflect the image of God in which each of us is created; to be a Christ-presence in the world?

Is this what Paul meant when he wrote, 'Do not be conformed to this world, but be transformed by the renewing of your minds' (Romans 12:2)?

You called them friends

You called them friends—
  That ill-assorted bunch.

Four fishermen:
  one with a foot-shaped mouth
  and a gentle, evangelistic brother;
    two fiery 'Sons of Thunder',
      one of whom was also called 'Beloved';
a tax collector, outcast and despised;
  a zealous extremist, and one
  recalled for introducing you to others;
    two whose integrity demanded proof
      before they could believe;
        another two whose names are all we know;
          the one who, having shown such promise,
          betrayed you with a kiss.

Unlikely characters
  to form your inner circle;
  to be entrusted
    with the future of your mission.

Perhaps there's hope for me
        because
  you called them friends.

Read John 15:15–16:

'I do not call you servants any longer, because the servant does not know what the master is doing; but I have called you friends, because I have made known to you everything that I have heard from my Father. You did not choose me but I chose you. And I appointed you to go and bear fruit, fruit that will last, so that the Father will give you whatever you ask him in my name.'

What does it mean to be a friend?

What do you do with a friend?

Maureen Halpin, in her book *Puddles of Knowing*,[7] tells of asking a group of young children, 'How do you know when someone loves you?' Several children spoke of playing games together, going for a bike ride, sharing toys and so on. Then one child said, 'When you got a real friend, you do a lot of nothing together.'

Deep friendship is not dependent on activity or conversation—though these may be valued aspects of it. Shared silence is often a significant feature. Just being together is enough.

Bring to mind someone whom you consider a close friend. What do you most value about them—and do you know what they most value about you?

How does it feel to know Jesus calls you 'Friend'?

How much time do you spend building this friendship?

How much time do you spend 'doing a lot of nothing together'? What might that involve?

Sacrament of care

'Give her something to eat,' he said,
as if she had awoken from ordinary sleep.
And yet we knew, beyond all doubt,
her sleep had been the sleep of death
from which no one returns.

'Give her something to eat!'
So simple and so sensible—
after such a journey she has no strength.
What has she seen and known?
Where has she been?

'Give her something to eat!'
Those words keep ringing in my ears;
stir me to action; bid me leave her side.
Preparing for my child the nourishment she needs
assumes a new significance.

'Give her something to eat!'
Never again will I prepare a meal or sweep a floor;
not make a bed or light the cooking fire
without those words, that voice, re-echoing.
He made a sacrament of what had been a chore.

Read Mark 5:22–24, 35–43 slowly and carefully.

Let your God-given imagination place you in the scene.

- Who are you?
- Where are you?
- Why are you there?
- What are you feeling as the drama unfolds?

In the midst of the wonder and rejoicing, you hear Jesus say, 'Give her something to eat' and you know that the words are addressed to you.

- What is your innermost response?
- How do you feel about leaving those gathered in celebration as you go to perform a mundane task?
- How does this reflect your attitude to daily chores?

Into a situation where life has been wondrously restored comes the call to sustain that life by the ordinary, everyday task of food preparation. The miraculous and the mundane, hand in hand, provide for the fullness of life. Both are equally valid; both are equally necessary; both are expressions of the presence of God.

Is there some responsibility, task or chore that you resent?

What difference might it make if you heard Jesus calling you to it?

What might a change in your attitude do for God?

Find and reflect on George Herbert's hymn 'Teach me, my God and King'.[8]

Do you know... ?

'Do you know what I have done for you?'
Those words, though whispered to another,
rang in my ears… and rang… and rang again
with every repetition.

To each one they were spoken;
from each, response required.
The time approached when they'd be said to me
and I would have to answer.

The waiting seemed like all eternity…
and yet the moment came too soon!
I knew I was not ready—never would be—
as you, with towel and basin, knelt before me.

You gently washed my feet, and gently dried them;
then spoke the words I dreaded—longed—to hear.
'My dear one, do you know
what I have done for you?'

I want to cry aloud, 'Of course I do!'
The words die on my lips—
for my heart knows that I can never
fully comprehend the truth.

There are no words for answer—
only tears.

In many churches, the observance of Maundy Thursday includes a ritual washing of feet or hands as the actions of Jesus are recalled. Like any ritual, this can be, at worst, an empty 'going through the motions' or, at best, a profound, challenging, even transformative experience.

Read John 13:3–17.

Now read it slowly again, one sentence at a time, and let imagination place you among those gathered in the upper room. Use all your senses to experience the event.

- As you look around, whom do you recognise?
- Where is Jesus? Where are you?
- What can you feel, smell, taste, see and hear?
- What are you thinking?
- Why are you here?

The buzz of conversation fades as Jesus, a towel tied round his waist and carrying a bowl of water, kneels before someone on the far side of the room and washes their feet. How do the people around you react? What are they murmuring? How does the atmosphere in the room change?

Jesus begins to move from person to person, washing the feet of each in turn, and you watch how each one responds. Now you realise that soon he will kneel before you and wash your feet. What is your inner response?

The moment arrives—and you feel him gently lift one of your feet into the cool, refreshing water, wash it, then gently fold it in the towel and dry it. Now the other foot. Does he say anything? Do you? What are you feeling, thinking?

Journal your experience. What have you discovered?

Good Friday

Another Friday. Another ordinary day.
  Roman soldiers go about their duties,
  carry out distasteful orders
  obedient in their execution.

Another ordinary day on Golgotha.
  Three more troublemakers,
  disturbers of the peace, held high
  for all to see the wages of their sins.

Events dividing history into 'before' and 'after'
  always occur on ordinary days.
  Hiroshima, Chernobyl, September the Eleventh—
  most of the world lived these

      as

    just another ordinary day.

Crucifixion was nothing unusual in Roman-occupied territories, so for most people this was 'just another ordinary day'. In a time when news travelled slowly, even most of those whose lives had been touched by Jesus would have been unaware of what was happening.

In his painting *Christ of Saint John of the Cross*, Salvador Dali presents a God's-eye view of the crucifixion. Seen from above, the figure of Jesus on the cross dominates the dark canvas, filling the space between earth and heaven. Right at the bottom of the picture, a group of fishermen go about their daily business of mending nets and preparing to launch their boats—oblivious to the event that, for many, would divide history into 'before and after'.

What are the 'before and after' events (delightful or painful) in your own life journey?

Which one calls for your attention today?

Take time to become part of this event once more. What is most vivid about it?

Are you willing and able to thank God for what has evolved from this event or does something need to be healed before you can do so?

Spend time reflecting on this in God's presence.

Jesus said, 'Unless a grain of wheat falls into the earth and dies, it remains just a single grain; but if it dies, it bears much fruit' (John 12:24).

Resurrection

To those with eyes to see,
  evidence of resurrection
  is everywhere.
    It is the basic principle
      by which the cosmos operates.

Energy exploding from the primal fireball
  can never be destroyed.
  It manifests itself in different forms
    which last but for a while—
      for all is stardust
        and to stardust will return.

Stars and galaxies appear,
  live out their time, then die.
  The energy of each new thing
    emerging into being
      has previously been expressed
        in other forms.

The sub-atomic particles
  vibrating in the atoms of my body
  have been vibrating since the dawn of time.
    I wonder at the stories they might tell
      of other incarnations.

To those with eyes to see,
  evidence of resurrection
  is everywhere.

Without death there can be no new beginning. The transformation of energy from one expression to another is foundational to life in all its forms. Everything that dies releases energy essential for new life. Nothing is lost; nothing is wasted; nothing is without purpose; always there is transformation. 'Without extinction the dance of life is fundamentally incomplete.'[9]

Stories of encounters with Jesus after his crucifixion speak of this. Repeatedly he was unrecognised until some word or action sparked awareness of his presence; repeatedly the limitations of physicality were breached as he appeared and disappeared (Luke 24:13–53; John 20).

When he was at table with them, he took bread, blessed and broke it, and gave it to them. Then their eyes were opened, and they recognised him; and he vanished from their sight.
LUKE 24:30–31

Think back over your life. What have you lost? What died—a dream, hope, relationship, treasured pet or person? Let yourself feel the loss—then explore what change or growth has occurred that might not have been possible without it.

Can you find signs of new life, of resurrection, of transformation for which to give thanks?

If not, are you willing to seek for the hidden gift that waits to be discovered?

How can you celebrate this?

Holy fire

Tongues of fire;
tokens of God's presence;
reminders of a flaming bush—
on fire but not consumed.

The Spirit settling now upon each one,
empowering, bestowing gifts
of courage, of communication
and of understanding.

This flame that drives us out
to spread the gospel message,
to face the pain of persecution and rejection,
sometimes feels like hell.

Can it be possible
the fire of hell and of the Spirit
are, in truth, the same?

Fire brings warmth and comfort, but fire can also bring pain and destruction; it is used to cook nourishing food and to burn rubbish; it is used to bring healing and to purify and it is used to inflict pain—sometimes simultaneously. Fire is both a creative force, shaping the earth through volcanic activity, and a destructive one—as in forest fire.

Rudolf Otto says:

> *The truly 'mysterious'… is beyond our apprehension and our comprehension… In it we come upon something 'wholly other'… before which we recoil in a wonder that strikes us chill and numb… It shows itself as something uniquely attractive and fascinating… The daunting and the fascinating combine in a strange harmony of contrasts.*[10]

Throughout scripture, God's presence in fire, usually associated with a call and commissioning, is experienced in this way. Moses, attracted to the sight of the bush that burned without being consumed (Exodus 3:3), hid his face for fear of God (v. 6); John the Baptist promised a baptism with fire (Matthew 3:11), a promise fulfilled at Pentecost (Acts 2:1–4) with a call to spread the gospel—a call to privilege, pain and persecution.

Looking back over your own life, try to recall some experience of pain or distress that felt, at the time, like 'going through hell'. Can you now, with the advantage of hindsight, recognise the presence of the One who burns with holy fire—calling you to new awareness, new understanding, new growth, new life and perhaps new ministry?

Spend some time in the presence of that daunting and fascinating Holy Mystery.

Journal your experience.

Pondering

The labyrinth

Great ring of riverstone and gentle grass,
mysterious ancient symbol, pilgrim pathway,
emerging from the earth where you have lain in secret,
concealed from sight until the time was ripe
for your delivery into the light of day—
to reawaken consciousness in us.

Serpentine, sinuous, your path leads on.
Faithful walking, only, will bring me to your centre
named for the new Jerusalem—
that place where peace and wholeness may be found;
where I discover wisdom, strength and courage
to face the issues of my own life journey.

Reviresco.[11]
Sacred space.
I grow green again.

The origins of labyrinths are lost in the mists of time, but for thousands of years they have been a part of almost every religious tradition. An early Christian labyrinth with the words *Sancta Ecclesia* ('Holy Church') at the centre is part of a fourth-century Christian site in Algeria.

Unlike a maze (which has multiple paths from which choices must be made), a labyrinth has a single path that winds its way to the centre. The same path leads the walker back out.

During the Crusades, when it was too dangerous for pilgrims to visit the Holy Land, several European cathedrals were designated as centres of pilgrimage. Here pilgrims could walk a labyrinth, rest in the central space (often called 'the New Jerusalem') and return to the world refreshed by time spent in a holy place.

It seems that the time has come for this ancient symbol of the spiritual journey to be restored so that today's walkers may rediscover the power of pilgrimage and of a walking meditation in sacred space, where everything that happens can be received as metaphor. Some scripture texts that have been applied to the labyrinth include:

When you turn to the right or when you turn to the left, your ears shall hear a word behind you, saying, 'This is the way; walk in it.'
ISAIAH 30:21

'Enter through the narrow gate; for the gate is wide and the road is easy that leads to destruction, and there are many who take it. For the gate is narrow and the road is hard that leads to life, and there are few who find it.'
MATTHEW 7:13–14

Of course, walking the beach or some other significant pathway can serve the same purpose if done with awareness of God's presence and openness to God's revelation.

When did you last consciously go for a walk with God? Why not schedule a time to do so?

On walking a labyrinth

As I step out to journey on a new old path
I find it soft and gentle to my feet;
beckoning, inviting, calling me to dare
to trust myself to walk where it shall lead—
whatever the terrain.

This time I'm ready to accept the invitation.
This time I can, with eagerness, step out.
This time is kairos time;
the appointed time when all things come together;
a moment when the spirit stirs—
    and my own spirit knows
the hour has come.

It is often when life is comfortably settled that the call comes to journey on, to seek once more the gifts and challenges of an unknown future. Some inner wisdom recognises that accepting the invitation means nothing will ever be the same again, while saying 'No' will mean living with the loss of all that might have been.

In the face of such a choice, it is prudent to take time to listen, to reflect, and to avoid foolishly rushing in where angels fear to tread. (See Luke 14:28–33, where Jesus talks about the need to count the cost of our actions.)

Walking a labyrinth is one way to honour such threshold times. As the path leads in one direction, then another, towards the centre and back out to the perimeter, our hopes and fears, dreams and doubts may become clearer. Bodily experience joins with head and heart in the process of discernment.

Take time, now, to revisit and list threshold experiences in your own life, to feel and name all that you felt then.

What enabled you to make your choice?

Are there choices you now regret? Share them with God and journal your conversation. Does anything surprise you?

If possible, walk a labyrinth with these issues as your focus or, if no labyrinth is available, walk on a beach or some familiar pathway.

Walking a familiar path

I've walked this pathway many times before.
I've come to recognise each convolution;
they mark familiar turning points
on many explorations.

Each time I walk, it is a new adventure
leading… I know not where.
Though each experience is different
the path remains the same.

I know the labyrinth will offer me some gift
if I can only recognise and claim it—
maybe a new awareness, or an insight,
perhaps an invitation, or an answer,
a question I have never asked before
to open up my heart and feed my soul.

And so I come again, with expectation;
take off my shoes, for this is holy ground.
Barefoot, I step on to the path—
and walk where Wisdom's Spirit hovers.

Is there not something inviting about a familiar path? The sense of recognition and reassurance of arrival at a known destination can be both gift and trap.

How delightful it can be to journey down a path so familiar that there is no need to focus on its surface or direction. Instead there is freedom to notice other things—the freshness of the air laden with perfume of the local environment, the rising questions or celebrations of one's own heart, awe at the wonder of creation in all its power.

How easy it is to travel a well-known route barely aware of the surrounding territory, seeing only what has always been seen, virtually oblivious to everything else. This can be true of relationships with both people and God: familiarity can indeed breed contempt. Favourite hymns, prayers and styles of worship can all become blocks to exploration of something new and fresh, which may lead to growth.

In the story of the sower (Matthew 13:1–9), the pathways were unable to accept or nurture the seed of new life.

What are the well-trodden pathways in your life?

What are the unconsidered patterns of thought, word and deed; the automatic reactions in unguarded moments, which limit fullness of humanity?

Can these same familiar pathways be explored afresh for gifts and treasures hidden beneath the surface?

What are the familiar things and places that set you free to meet more deeply with God?

Return to the centre

Stillness, silence—
intense beyond description—
embrace, enfold,
welcome the traveller returned
from too long sojourning in distant lands.

I had not recognised my wandering;
nor understood the restless seeking,
the emptiness no action ever filled,
the deep dissatisfaction, ngakau[12] pain.

Now stillness, silence—
intense beyond description—
embrace, enfold, and heal.

Have you ever experienced that place of deep inner stillness where silence wraps itself around you like a cloak; that place where all thoughts and distractions fall away and you know, beyond all doubt, that you have touched the heart of God, that you have come home?

How hard it is to carry that sense of inner stillness and peace back into the busyness of everyday life! How easy to be drawn back on to the treadmill of old routines and striving to meet the expectations of doing rather than being! Somewhere, deep within, lurks the knowledge that these patterns will never bring real satisfaction or happiness.

Labyrinth pilgrims recognise the central space as a place of provision, a holy place to which they have been led, a place of resting in green pasture, beside still waters; a place where the soul is restored (Psalm 23:2–3). To rest here until called to journey on, to return to the cares and concerns of everyday life, is to gather strength and wisdom for whatever challenges may lie ahead—even traversing 'the valley of the shadow of death' (v. 4). To revisit the centre is to renew spiritual energy.

Review your life journey by slowly reading Psalm 23 and relating each verse to some remembered time or situation.

Give thanks for times of healing and restoration.

Where there is healing still required, or where there is doubt or uncertainty, make a time to bring it to the God who dwells in the depth of your innermost being.

Credo

If you would know
What really is believed,
Heed not what is professed.

Study instead
the attitudes and actions,
priorities and practice;
the way of life;
integrity of being.

In these is shown
the truth
about relationship with God.

How easy it is to recite creeds and dogmas, to parrot words learned in childhood, to state 'I believe…' without stopping to examine the content of the statement. Even if time is taken for reflection, 'I believe…' is often understood as 'To this I give intellectual assent', while its root meaning is more like 'To this I totally commit myself.'

Surely what *really* is believed is shown in daily life. Actions speak louder than words. Francis of Assisi is thought to have told his brothers to 'proclaim the gospel and, if necessary, even use words'. Many people know only too well the businessman who is a pillar of the church on Sunday, yet engages in dubious, if not dishonest, practices on Monday.

In Matthew 7:21–23 we read:

> *'Not everyone who says to me, "Lord, Lord", will enter the kingdom of heaven, but only one who does the will of my Father in heaven. On that day many will say to me, "Lord, Lord, did we not prophesy in your name, and cast out demons in your name, and do many deeds of power in your name?" Then I will declare to them, "I never knew you; go away from me, you evil doers."'*

How do these words speak into your life? What does their spotlight reveal?

In his poem 'As kingfishers catch fire', Gerard Manley Hopkins comments on the way in which the true nature of all things is revealed ('What I do is me… The just man justices…'). Find and read this poem.[13] Do you agree with Hopkins? Why or why not?

How well do your thoughts, words and actions reflect what you claim to believe?

Notes

1   From 'Domestic poem' by Eileen Moeller (2008).
2   'Auguries of innocence' by William Blake (1803).
3   William Blake (1794).
4   One of the many beaches on the North Shore of the Waitemata harbour, Auckland, Aotearoa/New Zealand.
5   Exodus 33:20.
6   Michael Riddell, *Threshold of the Future* (SPCK, 1998), p. 125.
7   Maureen Halpin, *Puddles of Knowing* (William C. Brown, 1984), p. 23.
8   No. 337 in *Hymns Ancient and Modern* (revised 1991)
9   Diarmuid O'Murchu, *Quantum Theology* (Crossroad, 1997), p. 180.
10 Rudolf Otto, *The Idea of the Holy* (Oxford University Press, 1950), pp. 28, 31.
11 *Reviresco* (meaning 'I grow green again') is the name of a labyrinth at Twyford, near Hastings, in Aotearoa's (New Zealand's) Hawkes Bay. The design is that of the labyrinth built into the floor of Chartres cathedral (France) in the twelfth century.
12 *Ngakau* is the Maori word for centre, core, heart.
13 Available online at www.poetryfoundation.org/poem/173654.

Acknowledgments

Among the many who have supported and encouraged this project, the following must be acknowledged:

Vaughan Park Anglican Retreat and Conference Centre at Long Bay, Auckland, Aotearoa/NZ. It was during three months here in 2008 as Residential Scholar that the work was conceived, and here that I have been sheltered and nurtured throughout its gestation. Special thanks are due to the Director, the Revd John Fairbrother, and the Administrator, Marion Nickerson.

The Rt Revd David Rice, current bishop of my home diocese of Waiapu, for his generous interest and encouragement to continue exploring the horizons of my faith; for assuring me that I am not heretical; for writing the foreword.

The Revd Dr John Franklin, who, over many years, has helped me reflect on my experience of Holy Presence and find language to express it.

Alison and John Kerr, who were instrumental in my initial application for a Vaughan Park Scholarship, who provided me with a hermitage in which to read, reflect and write, and whose labyrinth 'Reviresco' has been a source of much inspiration.

My editor, Naomi Starkey, for her skilful and gentle midwifery as together we have brought this book to birth. To her and to her team at BRF, my heartfelt gratitude.

The Sacred Place of Prayer

The human person created in God's image

Jean Marie Dwyer, OP

Prayer is not a complicated set of methods or exercises, but as simple as living life, being ourselves and bringing God into our daily routine. Because we are all created in God's image, each of us is the privileged and sacred place of prayer.

Drawing on scripture, the desert tradition, great spiritual figures from history and the author's own Dominican tradition, this book explores the various steps we need to take to nurture our life in God. After laying the philosophical, biblical and theological groundwork, Sister Jean Marie Dwyer goes on to offer rich insights into how we find our true self and our place of belonging.

ISBN 978 0 85746 241 1   £7.99
Available from your local Christian bookshop or, in case of difficulty, direct from BRF: please visit www.brfonline.org.uk.

Encircling the Christian Year

Liturgies and reflections
for the seasons of the Church

Barbara Mosse

The seasons of the Church's year parallel those of the natural world, gifting us with opportunities for spiritual life and growth. The watchfulness of Advent with its symbolism of light and darkness gives way to the explosion of joy as we welcome the birth of Christ; the sombre season of Lent leads us through the despair of the cross to the wonder and joy of Easter; and the weeks of 'Ordinary Time' encourage us to persist in our walk with Christ during those times when nothing much seems to be happening.

Beginning with Advent Sunday, *Encircling the Christian Year* presents a series of short liturgies for each week of the Church calendar, including a Bible reading, reflection and prayers, suitable for both individual and small group use. Special liturgies are also provided for the major festivals and 'red letter days'. The book invites us to deeper prayer, to grow in our relationship with the God who loves us and accompanies us through all the seasons of our lives.

ISBN 978 0 85746 045 5   £9.99
Available from your local Christian bookshop or, in case of difficulty, direct from BRF: please visit www.brfonline.org.uk.

Creating Community

Ancient ways for modern churches

Simon Reed

There is much talk today of 'new ways of being church' and 'new monastic spirituality'. As Simon Reed explored the Celtic roots of the Christian faith, in community with others who drew inspiration from our spiritual ancestors in the British Isles, he came to realise that the third-millennium church has much in common with the first-millennium church and, more importantly, much to learn from it.

In *Creating Community*, he introduces us to a new but at the same time very old way of being church which is based upon three core elements: a Way of Life, a network of Soul Friends, and a rhythm of prayer. The book shows how the rediscovery of these elements by Christians today offers a vital key that opens up an ancient way for modern churches, one that not only helps to bring believers to lasting maturity but creates genuine and much-needed community in an increasingly fragmented world.

ISBN 978 0 85746 009 7   £7.99
Available from your local Christian bookshop or, in case of difficulty, direct from BRF: please visit www.brfonline.org.uk.

Restoring the Woven Cord

Strands of Celtic Christianity for the Church today

Michael Mitton

When they discover Celtic spirituality, many Christians feel that in some sense they have come home. As they begin to explore the people and places significant in the early centuries of Christianity in the British Isles, they find an expression of faith that weaves together strands of being and belonging, worship and witness in a unique and powerful way.

Restoring the Woven Cord takes 15 leading figures from that era—ranging from Patrick of Ireland to John of Beverley—and shares something of their stories, showing their burning love for the Bible, their depth of prayer, their radical commitment to the poor and to caring for creation. Reflecting on their lives and works, we can find powerful inspiration for our own walk with God and rich resources for the ministry of the local church.

This is a revised edition of a bestselling book first published in 1995.

ISBN 978 0 1 84101 800 3   £8.99
Available from your local Christian bookshop or, in case of difficulty, direct from BRF: please visit www.brfonline.org.uk.

Servant Ministry

A portrait of Christ and a pattern for his followers

Tony Horsfall

Servanthood is something to which all believers are called, not just those in full-time ministry. This means that understanding what servanthood means is vital for the health and well-being of local churches. Every member needs to appreciate their role as a servant of God. At the same time, the principles of servant-leadership provide an essential framework for those called specifically to the work of the church, whether at home or overseas.

Servant Ministry offers a practical exposition of the first 'Servant Song' in Isaiah (42:1–9). Writing from many years of Christian teaching and mentoring, Tony Horsfall applies insights drawn from the Isaiah passage to topics such as the motivation for service and the call to serve; valid expressions of servanthood and the link between evangelism and social action; character formation and what it means to be a servant; how to keep going over the long haul in the harsh realities of ministry; the importance of listening to God on a daily basis and also over a whole lifetime.

ISBN 978 0 85746 088 2   £7.99
Available from your local Christian bookshop or, in case of difficulty, direct from BRF: please visit www.brfonline.org.uk.

The Recovery of Love

Walking the Way of Wholeness

Naomi Starkey

'... *Washed flat and almost clean by the ebb of the tide, the sand is bare except for a single set of footprints. And—why are we not surprised?—there he is again, ahead of us, waiting. Although it is barely dawn, there is light enough to see his face, recognise his smile. The shadows have gone, for this in-between time, anyway. When he speaks, we know his voice, although we cannot place his accent. Five words; a question: "What do you really want?"'*

Some people like to be taken on mystery tours; others prefer to know where they are going, how long it will take, and where they will stop for lunch. This book is a bit of a mystery tour, exploring aspects of faith and truth through storytelling and reflection on the Bible. At its heart is the meaning of love: on the one hand, our hunger for it and often weary search to find it, and on the other hand God's breathtaking love for us.

ISBN 978 1 84101 892 8   £6.99
Available from your local Christian bookshop or, in case of difficulty, direct from BRF: please visit www.brfonline.org.uk.

Enjoyed

this book?

Write a review—we'd love to hear what you think.
Email: reviews@brf.org.uk

Keep up to date—receive details of our new books as they happen.
Sign up for email news and select your interest groups at:
www.brfonline.org.uk/findoutmore/

Follow us on Twitter @brfonline

By post—to receive new title information by post (UK only), complete the form below and post to: BRF Mailing Lists, 15 The Chambers, Vineyard, Abingdon, Oxfordshire, OX14 3FE

Your Details
Name _____
Address_____
_____
Town/City _____ Post Code _____
Email_____

Your Interest Groups (*Please tick as appropriate)	
☐ Advent/Lent	☐ Messy Church
☐ Bible Reading & Study	☐ Pastoral
☐ Children's Books	☐ Prayer & Spirituality
☐ Discipleship	☐ Resources for Children's Church
☐ Leadership	☐ Resources for Schools

Support your local bookshop
Ask about their new title information schemes.